WAITING
for
CHRISTMAS

Stories and Activities for Advent

By CAROL GREENE

Illustrated by ELIZABETH SWISHER

Copyright © 1987 Augsburg Publishing House

LCCC 87-070474   ISBN 0-8066-2264-4

Manufactured in the U.S.A.   APH 10-6915

1 2 3 4 5 6 7 8 9

AUGSBURG Publishing House • Minneapolis

A Note to Parents & Friends of Children

Advent is a time of preparation and a time of waiting. Children may find it especially hard to wait for Christmas to come. This book of stories, activities, prayers, poems, and songs was written to help families wait and to suggest some ways to prepare for the celebration of our Savior's birth.

The weeks before Christmas can be packed with last-minute shopping and baking and cleaning. Sometimes, in the midst of all our preparations, we can lose sight of the importance of Christmas—the coming to earth of God's own Son. Take time to meet around an Advent wreath and pray, or make a Jesse tree, or read a story, or sing a song or two. Help your child to understand Advent and Christmas.

Advent is also a time of joyful expectation. God's promise of a Savior is told in a variety of forms—in poems, stories, and song. Also included are humorous selections to delight young ears and encourage happy hearts. Activities for the family and easy-to-do projects will help speed along the time of waiting.

Enjoy waiting for Christmas with your child!

The Editor

For Eileen

2

Waiting for Christmas

I'm waiting for Christmas.
My mind's in a spin
Of angels and shepherds,
No room at the inn.

I'm waiting for Christmas.
My mind's in a muddle
Of fields and a stable
Where animals huddle.

I'm waiting for Christmas.
My mind's in a jumble
Of Mary and Joseph,
The baby so humble.

I'm waiting for Christmas.
My mind's not to blame.
Oh, what did folks wait for
Before Christmas came?

The Promise

This way, Becca!" called the boy. "I think it's in the ditch over here."

"Wait, Ben!" His sister hurried after him. "Let me help you."

The two children stood at the edge of the ditch. Below them lay a lamb, caught in a thornbush.

"I'll go down and free it," said the boy. "Then I'll hand it up to you."

It wasn't an easy job. The frightened lamb kicked and squirmed. But at last they got it out of the ditch.

"Whew!" said the boy. "My arms are covered with scratches. The lamb's got some on its face too. We'd better take it home with us. Grandfather has some salve."

"I cut my leg on a rock," said the girl. "What a rotten day. I'm *ready* to go home."

It didn't take their grandfather long to put salve on the scratches and a bandage on the girl's leg.

"There!" he said. "You'll all be fine. But you'll have to take the lamb back to its mother, you know."

"Rats!" said the boy. "I'm tired."

"I know." The old man sighed. "I wish you children didn't have to work so hard. I wish I could do more. But I'm just too old to climb those hills anymore."

"It's all right." The girl patted his hand. "Do you

know what I wish, though? I wish there was someone to look after us—all of us—the way we look after the sheep."

"Someday there will be, Becca." Grandfather smiled. "Someday God will send a shepherd for us. God promised. That's what the prophets say."

"A shepherd?" repeated the boy. "What will he be like?"

Grandfather hobbled over to the door and looked out. He was still smiling.

"He will feed his flock—his people—like a shepherd. He'll carry the lambs in his arms. Indeed, he'll love those sheep so much that he'll give his life for them, to keep them safe forever."

"*God* promised that?" asked the boy.

"Yes, Ben, he did," said the old man. "And God will keep his promise. Just wait."

"A shepherd for people. That's quite a promise." Suddenly the boy didn't look tired anymore. "Well, time to get that lamb back to its mother. Coming, Becca?"

"Coming," said the girl. But she stopped for a moment at the door and hugged her grandfather. "A good shepherd who will love us forever," she whispered. "Yes, that's worth waiting for."

Candles, Greens, & Memories

People first made Advent wreaths in Germany many years ago. Today's wreaths can be anything from a simple circle of wire with greenery attached and four candle holders to a ceramic or metal wreath bought at a religious supplies store.

Most people light one candle on the first Sunday of Advent (four Sundays before Christmas). Then they add the second candle on the second Sunday, and so on. Sometimes all four candles are purple. Purple reminds us of two things: that we are sorry for our sins and that Jesus is a royal king. Some people use a pink candle for the third Sunday, which is supposed to be more joyful.

Often families have a little worship service or say a prayer together as they light the candles. They remember all the people who waited for the first Christmas. Sometimes, when Christmas finally comes, they put fresh white candles in the holders and thank God for the birth of his Son.

The First Candle

Like a candle long ago
Your promise, Lord, burned true.
You keep all your promises.
Keep *us* true to you.

John's Story

Zechariah and Elizabeth were old,
much too old to have children.
At least that's what folks thought.
Then one day Zechariah went to the temple.
There he saw the angel Gabriel.
Zechariah was scared.

"Fear not, Zechariah," said Gabriel.
"Elizabeth will have a son. Call him John."
Zechariah couldn't believe it.
"All right," said Gabriel.
"You won't be able to speak until the baby is born."
Sure enough, Zechariah couldn't speak.

Some time later, Elizabeth had her baby boy.
"How wonderful!" folks said.
"Of course you'll call him Zechariah."
"No," said Elizabeth. "John."
"Whoever heard such a thing?" folks said.
"What do you think, Zechariah?"

Zechariah grabbed a tablet.
"His name is John," he wrote.
At that moment, he could speak again.
"Blessed be the Lord," he said.
"He remembers his promise to save us.
And you, little child, will go before the Lord
and get people ready for him."

(Luke 1:5-25, 51-79)

7

The Jesse Tree

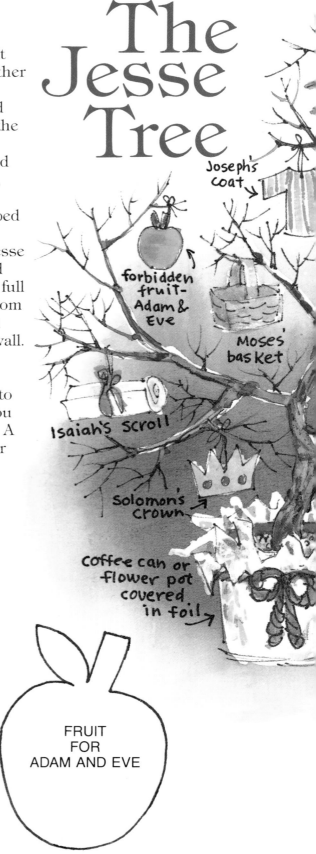

For years people have made Jesse trees as they wait for Christmas. The trees are named for Jesse, the father of King David. Both Jesse and David were Jesus' ancestors. A Jesse tree helps us remember them and the other people who went before Jesus and helped the world wait for his birth.

Some of those people, such as Abraham, Isaac, and Jacob, heard God's promise to send a savior. Others, such as Moses and David, trusted God to keep that promise. Still others, such as Mary and Joseph, helped the promise to be kept.

It doesn't matter what kind of tree you use for a Jesse tree. It can be a small evergreen tree or a large potted plant. A bare branch stuck in a bottle or a coffee can full of sand works well. You can cut a plain brown tree from a paper bag and tape it to the refrigerator. Or you can draw a tree on a big piece of paper and hang it on a wall.

What's important is how you decorate your Jesse tree. First, make a list of some of those people who went before Jesus. Use a Bible or a Bible storybook to help you. Then think of one thing that will remind you of each person, and make an ornament for each one. A basket might remind you of Moses. A saw or hammer would be good for Joseph, the carpenter. A rolled up strip of paper could be used for Isaiah, the prophet.

LAMB
FOR
DAVID

FRUIT
FOR
ADAM AND EVE

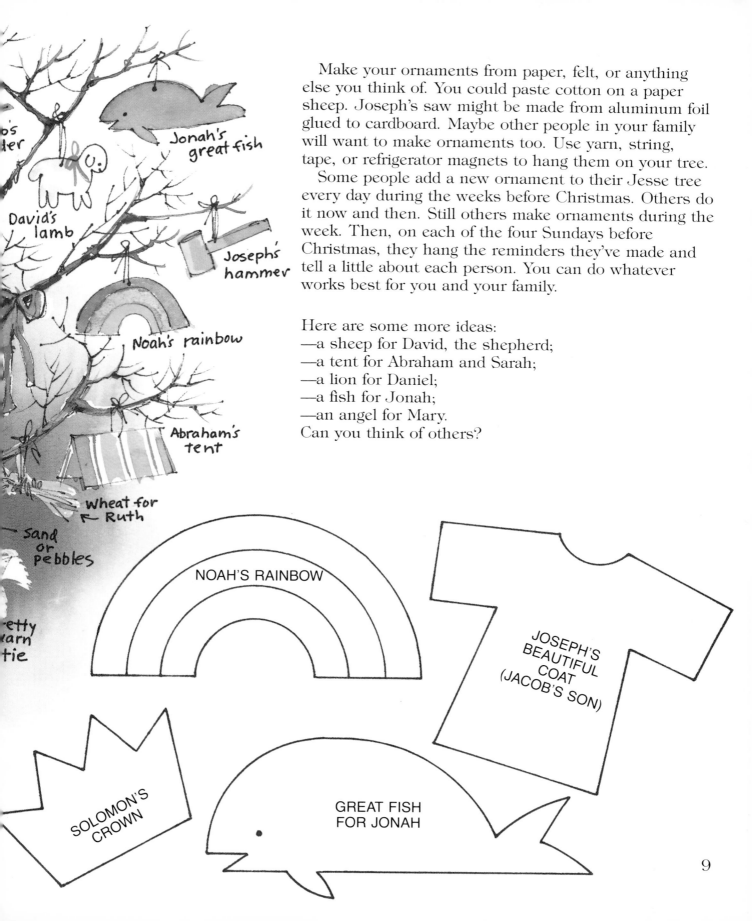

Make your ornaments from paper, felt, or anything else you think of. You could paste cotton on a paper sheep. Joseph's saw might be made from aluminum foil glued to cardboard. Maybe other people in your family will want to make ornaments too. Use yarn, string, tape, or refrigerator magnets to hang them on your tree.

Some people add a new ornament to their Jesse tree every day during the weeks before Christmas. Others do it now and then. Still others make ornaments during the week. Then, on each of the four Sundays before Christmas, they hang the reminders they've made and tell a little about each person. You can do whatever works best for you and your family.

Here are some more ideas:
—a sheep for David, the shepherd;
—a tent for Abraham and Sarah;
—a lion for Daniel;
—a fish for Jonah;
—an angel for Mary.
Can you think of others?

Jonah's great fish

David's lamb

Joseph's hammer

Noah's rainbow

Abraham's tent

Wheat for Ruth

sand or pebbles

etty arn tie

NOAH'S RAINBOW

JOSEPH'S BEAUTIFUL COAT (JACOB'S SON)

SOLOMON'S CROWN

GREAT FISH FOR JONAH

The List of Jeremy

Jeremy Quist
made a humongous list
of the Christmas gifts
he hoped to get.

It reached to the floor; it curled out the door . . . but Jeremy wasn't through yet.

"There's this and there's that
and a new baseball bat,
and a bright shiny something-or-other."

Jeremy Quist
did not notice the list had by now slithered over his mother.

Quist

and a green parakeet . . .

a robot . . .

"Pajamas with feet . . .

a race car . . .

a clown."

With a dip and a glide, the list slid outside . . . . and merrily rolled into town.

Licking its chops, it whizzed through the shops

and tied up a clerk just for fun.

11

Then it stopped with a lurch
in front of a church
and Jeremy saw what he'd done.

"I've got it all wrong!" he cried to the throng
of people who stared at that list.
"Why, where would we be if God were like me?
I'm sorry!" sobbed Jeremy Quist.

"God chose to give, so people could live.
Well, I'm going to start giving too.
My humongous list," said Jeremy Quist,

12

"I hereby donate to the zoo."

The Second Candle

In the past when times were dark,
Your Word shone bright as day.
Let it shine today for us,
And guide us on our way.

Tongue Twisters

Try to say these three times—*quickly:*

Absolutely zilch said silent Zechariah.
Jacob, Joseph, John, Josiah, join the Jesse tree.
We wish and we whisper while we wait for Christmas.
Surprised shepherds share celestial songs.

Mary's Story

Mary sat alone in her parents' home in Nazareth.
Soon she would marry Joseph, the carpenter.
They'd start a home and family of their own.

All at once, Mary wasn't alone anymore.
An angel stood before her, the angel Gabriel.
"Rejoice!" said the angel. "God is with you."

What does that *mean?* Mary wondered.
She was confused—and scared.

"Fear not, Mary," said Gabriel.
"You are going to have a baby.
You must call him Jesus.
He will rule over many people—forever."

Now Mary was really confused.
"But I don't have a husband," she said.
"How can I have a baby?"

"God will be the baby's father," said Gabriel.
"Nothing is impossible for God.
Why, your cousin, old Elizabeth,
is going to have a baby too."

Then Mary wasn't confused or scared anymore.
"I am God's servant," she said.
"I will do whatever God wants."

(Luke 1:26-38)

14

15

A Manger Full of Love

I remember when I was a girl—"
Grandma rolled out more cookie dough.

"Yes?" said Melanie. "Yes?" She loved to hear about the old days.

"I remember a custom my grandmother taught me." Grandma dusted her hands with flour. "She said the weeks before Christmas are a good time to think about God's love and to share it with others. She had me make a little manger from a box. 'Every time you share God's love with someone,' she said, 'put a piece of dried grass in the manger. It will help you remember how God shared his love for *you*

that first Christmas.' Maybe you would like to try the custom too, Melanie."

"I would!" said Melanie. "I'll start right now." She found a box, covered it with brown paper, and set it on the kitchen counter.

"There's my manger," she said. "Now, who can I share God's love with?"

Grandma thought awhile. "Why not take some cookies to Mrs. Kolowski?" she suggested. "Her arthritis is pretty bad. She'd probably be glad to get them."

So Melanie hurried next door with cookies. When she came back, she put one piece of dried grass in the manger.

"It sure isn't much of a bed yet," she sighed.

But as the weeks went by, she found many ways to share God's love. She set the table for her mother and sang her baby brother to sleep. She put a toy in the barrel for poor children, found Mr. Tucker's lost cat, and fed the birds every day.

"God loves birds too," she explained. Grandma nodded.

On Christmas Eve, Melanie thought of one more thing to do. She ran next door and recited her Christmas poem to Mrs. Kolowski. But when she came back with her piece of dried grass, the manger wasn't on the counter anymore.

I'll bet it got thrown away by accident, thought Melanie. Sadly she went to her room to get ready for church. Then she stopped and stared at the table by her bed. On it sat the manger, full of the dried grass she'd put in it. On top of the grass lay a baby.

"It's the same doll my grandmother gave me." Grandma stepped in from the hall and hugged her. "Merry Christmas, Melanie."

"Oh!" Melanie hugged her back. "Oh, thank you!" She looked at the doll again. "And thank *you,* God," she whispered.

(You can make and fill a manger too. If you can't find dried grass, cut colored paper into strips for straw.)

17

A Special Present

One good way to wait for Christmas is to make some of the gifts you plan to give. A book you've made yourself is always a special present, and a book that tells the story of Jesus' birth is even more special.

First decide how long you want your book to be. Sixteen pages plus a cover might be just right. Fold sheets of typing paper or construction paper in half to form the pages. (Each sheet will give you four pages.) If you want your cover to be a little different, use a spare piece of wallpaper or paste cloth or gift wrap on light-weight cardboard. Punch two holes at the fold of your book and tie the pages together with yarn or ribbon.

Here are some easy ways to draw people and things in the Christmas story.

BASIC FIGURE

MARY

ANGELS

SHEPHERD

JOSEPH

WISE MEN

On the first page, write your title for the story and your name. On the remaining pages, tell the story in your own words. Print your words at the bottom of the pages so you'll have plenty of room for pictures.

(Hint: If you have trouble getting started, pretend you are telling the story out loud to someone who has never heard it before. Then simply write down what you would say. Be sure to say something on each page—or set of facing pages—that makes you think of a picture.)

When you've finished writing, go back and draw pictures to go with your words.

BABY JESUS

DONKEY

STARS

SHEEP

The Third Candle

Like a spark in Mary's heart
Her joy burst into song.
Kindle, Lord, that spark in us
To praise you all day long.

RIDDLES

As I went from spot to spot,
I had to say "Fear not" a lot.
Who am I?

My husband couldn't say a word,
But still I knew the news he'd heard.
Who am I?

An angel told me while I dreamed
That things were not the way they seemed.
Who am I?

Better far than toys or tree,
God gave his own dear Son to me.
Who am I?

ANSWERS: The angel Gabriel, Elizabeth, Joseph, you.

Mary's Song

Mary went to visit her cousin Elizabeth.
"Elizabeth! It's Mary!" she called.
At once Elizabeth felt
the little baby inside her jump for joy.
"Oh, Mary!" she cried. "God loves you very much.
And he loves the baby you are going to have.
How happy you must be!"

Mary was happy, so happy that she began to sing:

"My heart praises God and my spirit is glad
because he has saved me.
He has remembered me,
even though I am not important.
From now on, everyone will see
what he has done for me.

"God is holy and kind to his people.
He scattered wicked folks
and made kings leave their thrones.
He made ordinary folks special
and gave hungry folks good things to eat.
But he didn't give rich folks anything.

"He promised long ago to save us
and he has kept his promise."

(Luke 1:39-55)

21

THE Murgdorps

The Murgdorps are frantic. The Murgdorps are wild.
Each tall Murgdorp parent, each small Murgdorp child
Adds its loud wail to the hullabaloo:
"Christmas is coming! There's so much to do!

"Buy some more presents. We're short forty-three.
Clean up the family room. Chop down the tree.
Polish the ornaments. See? They're hazy.
Christmas is coming and we're going crazy.

22

"Keep baking cookies. You know we need dozens.
Send off the cards to the out-of-town cousins.
Don't stop to think or to talk or have fun.
Christmas is coming! We'll never get done!

"String blinky lights up all over the house.
Shampoo the cat. Tie a bow on the mouse.
More decorations! More glitter! Be quick!
Christmas is coming and we're feeling sick."

Hush! Not a sound. All the Murgdorps are sleeping.
When they wake up, there'll be plenty of weeping.
Three days they've slept, which is really too long.
"Christmas is over? What *did* we do wrong?"

23

The Fourth Candle

In those who trusted you, dear Lord,
Your peace glowed strong and clear.
Fill us with the peace that comes
From knowing you are near.

Things to Make

Another good way to wait for Christmas is to make your own set of nativity figures. For a simple set, draw and cut figures from stiff paper, leaving a tab at the bottom of each. Then fold the tabs back and tape the figures into a shoebox stable.

Or collect different sizes and shapes of bottles and jars. Paint them tan. Then paint faces and clothes on them, or glue on clothes made from paper or cloth.

You can make your own "little town of Bethlehem" too. Cover empty boxes with brown paper or paint them brown. Add black rectangles cut from paper for windows and doors. Arrange the finished boxes to form a town—perhaps for under your Christmas tree.

25

Joseph's Story

Joseph, the carpenter, was a good man.
He wanted to marry Mary.
But then he saw that she was going to have a baby.
Joseph was surprised
and afraid to marry Mary.

Then he fell asleep and had a dream.
In it an angel spoke to him.
"Don't be afraid to marry Mary.
God is the father of her baby.
When he is born, you must call him Jesus.
He will save his people from their sins."

What a relief! thought Joseph.
Now I can marry Mary.

And that is exactly what he did.

(Matthew 1:18-25)

A Waiting Carol

(This carol can be sung to the tune of
"Oh, Come, Oh, Come, Emmanuel.")

Carol Greene

French Processional, 15th Cent.

1. In an-cient days the proph - ets spoke To com-fort lost and
2. To doubt-ing Zech - a - ri - ah came God's ho - ly an - gel
3. And then to Ma - ry, maid - en mild, The an - gel prom - ised
4. As Jo - seph won-dered what ____ to do, The an - gel brought him
5. So let us, as we count ____ the days, Pre - pare to join in

lone - ly folk: "God prom - is - es a Sa - vior to send.
to ____ pro-claim The birth of John, who would ____ some day
heav - en's Child. Then joy in Ma - ry burned ____ so strong,
com - fort too. "Your Ma - ry's child is God's ____ own son
songs ____ of praise With those who once in a - ges past

Refrain

His reign of love will nev - er end."
For Je - sus Christ pre - pare ____ the way.
She sang to God her tri - umph song.   Re-joice! Re-joice!
And earth's sal - va - tion has ____ be - gun."
Saw God's great prom - ise kept ____ at last."

God's in - fant Son Shall come to earth for ev - 'ry-one.

The Christmas Story

Mighty me!" said Caesar. "I'm ruler of the world.
Let's count how many people I rule."
And so the counting began.

"We must go to Bethlehem," said Joseph.
"We must be counted in my hometown."
"But the baby will soon be born," said Mary.
"I know," said Joseph. "I know."

They got to Bethlehem late.
The inn was already full.
"You can stay in the stable," said the innkeeper.
"I'm afraid that's all that's left."
"I understand," sighed Joseph. "Thank you."

They settled themselves in the stable
and there Mary's baby was born.
She wrapped him in strips of cloth,
as mothers did back then,
and laid him in a manger full of straw.
"Rest now, Mary," said Joseph.
"I will watch the child."
So Mary closed her eyes
and the dark night folded itself
like a blanket around the stable.

Close by, shepherds were tending their sheep.
Suddenly the sky filled with light
and an angel appeared.
The shepherds trembled and shook in their sandals.

"Fear not," said the angel. "I bring good news,
news to make the whole world joyful.
Today, in Bethlehem, your Savior is born!
He is the Lord, the one God promised,
and you will find him in a manger."

Then a great throng of angels appeared.
"Glory to God in heaven!" they sang.
"And peace to his people on earth."

"Let's go!" said the shepherds, and they ran
as fast as they could to Bethlehem.

There in the stable they found baby Jesus
and told what the angel had said.
Mary listened quietly and kept their words
like a treasure, deep in her heart.

And baby Jesus slept in the manger,
lost in the dreams that babies dream,
the small, helpless ruler of the world.

(Luke 2:1-20)

Christ Is Born!

Carol Greene

C.G.

1. Pluck the harp, Blow the horn,
2. An - gels sing Of his birth:
3. Shep - herds run Far and near.
4. Chil - dren shout, Drum - mers drum,

Ring __ the __ bells __ Christ is born!
Praise __ to __ God, __ Peace to earth!
Tell __ the __ world __ He is here!
All __ re - joice __ Christ has come!